The Bake Sale

Multiplying and Dividing

Tony Hyland

Publishing Credits

Editor
Sara Johnson

Editorial Director
Emily R. Smith, M.A.Ed.

Editor-in-Chief
Sharon Coan, M.S.Ed.

Creative Director
Lee Aucoin

Publisher
Rachelle Cracchiolo, M.S.Ed.

Image Credits

The author and publisher would like to gratefully credit or acknowledge the following for permission to reproduce copyright material: cover, Big Stock Photos; Title, Photodisc; p.4 (below), Photodisc; p.4 (above), Shutterstock; p.6, Photodisc; p.7, Corbis; p.8, Big Stock Photos; p.9, Elvele Images/Alamy; p.10, Corbis; p.11, Kevin Foy/Alamy; p.12, Jochen Tack/Alamy; p.13, Corbis; p.14, Visions of America, LLC/Alamy; p.15, Visions of America, LLC/Alamy; p.16, I Stock Photos; p.17, NYCFoto.com; p.18, Shutterstock; p.19, NYCFoto.com; p.20, Corbis; p.21, Stock Connection Blue/Alamy; p.22, Getty Images; p.23, Alex Segre/Alamy; p.24 (left), Photodisc; p.24 (right), Ken Welsh/Alamy; p.25, Alice McBroom; p.26 (above), Photodisc; p.26 (below left), Shutterstock; p.26 (below right), Big Stock Photos; p.27 (above), Big Stock Photos; p.27 (below right), Shutterstock; p.27 (below left), Corbis RF; p.29, Big Stock Photos

While every care has been taken to trace and acknowledge copyright, the publishers tender their apologies for any accidental infringement where copyright has proved untraceable. They would be pleased to come to a suitable arrangement with the rightful owner in each case.

Teacher Created Materials

5301 Oceanus Drive
Huntington Beach, CA 92649-1030
http://www.tcmpub.com
ISBN 978-0-7439-0894-8
© 2009 Teacher Created Materials Publishing
Reprinted 2010

Table of Contents

Giant Bake Sale!   4

What Will We Bake?   6

Grandpa's Recipe   9

Changing the Recipe   12

Buying the Ingredients   16

Back at Home   18

Selling the Famous Fruit Muffins   24

Problem-Solving Activity   28

Glossary   30

Index   31

Answer Key   32

Giant Bake Sale!

Our school is going to have a giant bake sale. The bake sale will raise money for new library books. I like to read, so I want to help. Maybe I could bake something to sell at the bake sale.

How Much Money?

Corey's school wants to raise $500.00 to buy new books. So far, $150.00 has been raised. How much more money do they need to raise?

I love baking. My grandpa used to be a **baker**. He still bakes tasty bread at home. On the weekends, Grandpa sometimes shows me how to make bread, too.

A baker working in 1965

LET'S EXPLORE MATH

Grandpa's **bakery** sold bread loaves for $2.00. How many bread loaves can you buy for:

a. $9.00? **b.** $12.00? **c.** $19.00?

What Will We Bake?

I asked Grandpa if he would help me bake some bread for the bake sale.

"Why don't we make my Famous Fruit Muffins instead?" Grandpa said.

"Great idea!" I said. "But you will need to help me. I haven't baked muffins before."

Grandpa's Famous Fruit Muffins

Grandpa said, "My **recipe** (REH-suh-pee) makes 12 dozen fruit muffins. That's 144 muffins. I used to bake the whole batch in the big bakery oven."

"But we can't fit 144 muffins in our oven!" I said.

The oven at Grandpa's bakery

LET'S EXPLORE MATH

Grandpa suggests baking 144 muffins. Write an **equation** (ee-KWAY-shuhn) to answer the following problem.

a. Grandpa can bake 12 muffins in each batch. How many batches does he need to make to get 144 muffins?

"Don't worry!' said Grandpa. "We'll just divide the recipe into batches. The 144 muffins divided by 3 batches equals 48 muffins in each batch."

"Great! We have 4 muffin tins that hold 12 muffins each, so that's perfect," I said.

$$144 \div 3 = 48$$

Grandpa's Recipe

First, Grandpa and I had to work out what **ingredients** (in-GREE-dee-uhnts) we needed. Grandpa showed me the recipe for the Famous Fruit Muffins that he used to make at his bakery. This is the recipe that makes 144 muffins.

Grandpa's Famous Fruit Muffins

Ingredients: (makes 144 muffins)

18 eggs

8 cups flour

8 cups sugar

8 cups butter (softened)

9 tsp. baking powder

21 ounces chopped dried apricots

21 ounces raisins

9 ounces ground almonds

Cooking Measurements

A cup is a unit used to measure volume.
   1 cup = 8 fluid ounces

What to Do:

- Preheat the oven to 350° F (180° C).

- Line the muffin tins with baking cups.

- Mix eggs, flour, sugar, butter, and baking powder in a large mixing bowl.

- Add the raisins, apricots, and ground almonds to bowl and stir.

- Put muffin mix into the 12-hole muffin tins.

- Bake muffins for 20 minutes or until golden brown.

- Take muffins out of oven and remove them from the tins.

- Leave muffins to cool.

LET'S EXPLORE MATH

A total of 18 eggs is needed to make 144 muffins! Which of the expressions below adds up to 18? *Hint:* Remember to work out the part in the parentheses (par-ENTH-es-eez) first!

a. $(3 \times 5) + 3$ **b.** $(1 \times 8) + 2$ **c.** $(6 \times 2) + 1$

A total of 21 ounces of raisins are needed. Which of the expressions below equals 21?

d. $(2 \times 7) + 9$ **e.** $(10 \times 2) + 1$ **f.** $(3 \times 8) + 2$

Changing the Recipe

"But that recipe shows how many ingredients are needed to make 144 muffins," I said to Grandpa. "We can only make 48 muffins at a time."

"So what do we need to do?" Grandpa asked me.

Grandpa's Famous Fruit Muffins

Ingredients: (makes 144 muffins)

18 eggs

8 cups flour

8 cups sugar

8 cups butter (softened)

9 tsp. baking powder

21 ounces chopped dried apricots

21 ounces raisins

9 ounces ground almonds

"Well, the recipe makes 144 muffins. And I can only cook 48 at a time. We have already worked out that I can make 3 batches of 48 muffins," I said.

$144 \div 48 = 3$ batches

I thought for a little while. "That means we need to divide the ingredient **amounts** by 3, too!"

"Well done!" said Grandpa.

First, I wrote down the old amounts. Then, I divided them each by 3.

Old Amounts

18 eggs	÷ 3	21 ounces chopped dried apricots	÷ 3
8 cups flour	÷ 3	21 ounces raisins	÷ 3
8 cups sugar	÷ 3	9 ounces ground almonds	÷ 3
8 cups butter (softened)	÷ 3		
9 tsp. baking powder	÷ 3		

LET'S EXPLORE MATH

Sometimes when we divide, the number we are dividing into does not divide evenly. For example, $8 \div 3$ does not divide into equal groups. There are some left over. These left over parts are called the remainder.

We can show $8 \div 3$ in a long division problem.

$$3 \overline{) \; 8}$$

How many groups of 3 are there in 8? There are 2 groups with 2 left over.

$$
\begin{array}{r}
2 \text{ R } 2 \\
3 \overline{) \; 8} \\
-6 \\
\hline
2
\end{array}
$$

Two groups of 3 is 6 with 2 remainder. The remainder is then written as a **fraction**.

So the answer is written as $2\frac{2}{3}$.

Then, I wrote down the new amounts needed to bake 24 muffins at a time.

New Amounts

6 eggs

2 ²/₃ cups flour

2 ²/₃ cups sugar

2 ²/₃ cups butter (softened)

3 tsp. baking powder

7 ounces chopped dried apricots

7 ounces raisins

3 ounces ground almonds

LET'S EXPLORE MATH

Use long division to work out the answers to these problems.

a. 10 ÷ 3

b. 12 ÷ 5

Buying the Ingredients

On the day before the bake sale, Grandpa arrived at my house early in the morning.

"Let's go to the market, Corey," he said. "We need to buy the ingredients."

I had decided to use $20.00 of my savings toward the ingredients. But I was worried it might not be enough.

"Don't worry," said Grandpa. "I'll lend you some money. I'm happy to help."

Grandpa gave me $30.00. We went to the store. It took a while, but we found all the ingredients we needed. And we had $15.00 left. I gave that $15.00 back to Grandpa.

Back at Home

It was time to start baking. "I think we can make 3 batches fairly easily," Grandpa said. "Clear the counters and the tabletop. We've got work to do."

First, Grandpa turned on the oven to warm it up. Then I measured the ingredients. I mixed them together in a bowl for the first batch.

How Many is a Dozen?

A dozen means 12. Eggs are usually sold by the dozen or half-dozen (6 eggs).

Corey and Grandpa are making 48 muffins at a time. Write at least 2 **multiplication** equations and at least 2 **division** equations using these numbers: 4, 6, 24, 48.

While I was mixing, Grandpa got out the muffin tins. They were shaped like rectangles.

"Four dozen muffins, coming up," said Grandpa. "Spoon the mixture into the tins, Corey."

At first, I thought the tins would not hold 12 muffins each. Each tin looked different. But then I looked closer. The tins were the same! It was just the way I looked at them.

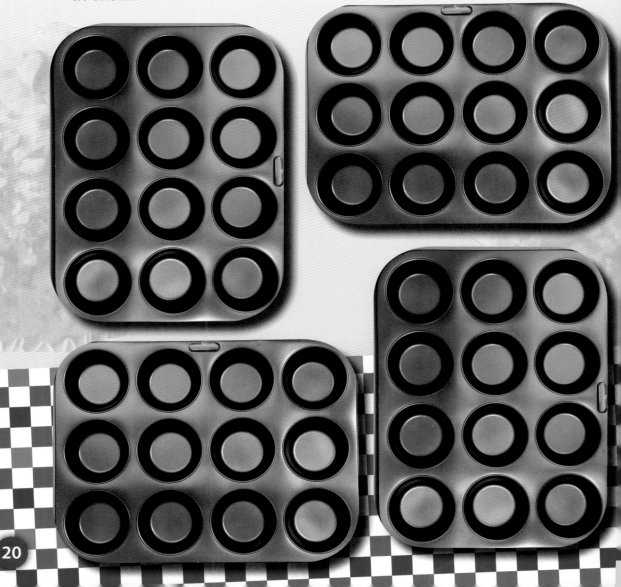

The first 2 tins held 12 muffins. They were set out in 3 rows of 4 muffin holes.

$3 \times 4 = 12$

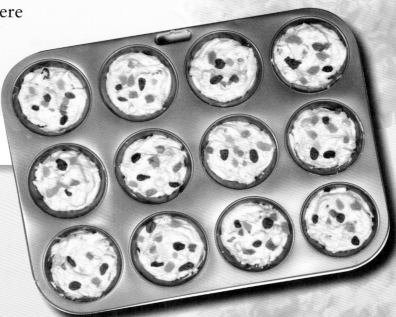

The other tins also held 12 muffins. They were set out in 4 rows of 3 muffin holes.

$4 \times 3 = 12$

Then Grandpa put the 4 tins into the oven.
After 40 minutes, the first batch of muffins was ready. Mom and Dad came into the kitchen to see how Grandpa and I were doing.

"You have 48 muffins made," said Mom. "How many more batches do you still need to cook?"

"There are still 2 batches to bake," I said. "Each batch has 48 muffins. So 2 multiplied by 48 equals 96 muffins still to bake!"

Dad laughed. "You had better keep baking," he said.

LET'S EXPLORE MATH

Corey and Grandpa have 2 batches of muffins still to bake. There are 48 muffins in each batch. They have cooked 1 batch of muffins already. Which expression below matches where they are in their cooking?

a. $(48 \times 2) + 2$ **b.** $(1 \times 48) + 2$ **c.** $(2 \times 48) + 48$

Selling the Famous Fruit Muffins

The next day at school was great. The Giant Bake Sale was amazing. I decided to sell Grandpa's Famous Fruit Muffins for $2.00 each. And they all sold out!

I was really happy. I had made $288.00. But I still owed Grandpa $15.00. And I had used $20.00 of my savings to buy ingredients.

Grandpa's Famous Fruit Muffins

~~$2 each~~

SOLD OUT!

LET'S EXPLORE MATH

Corey sold his muffins for $2.00 each. He sold all 144 muffins. So, he made $288.00.

a. If Corey had sold his muffins for $3.00 each, how much money would he have made?

b. If Corey had sold his muffins for $2.50 each, how much money would he have made?

From the total of $288.00, I subtracted $20.00. That went back into my savings. Then I subtracted the $15.00 I owed Grandpa. That left $253.00 to give to the school to buy new library books!

I felt really proud. In a few weeks, my school library would have new books. And now, at school, I was famous for making Grandpa's Famous Fruit Muffins.

LET'S EXPLORE MATH

Corey made $288.00. He subtracted his **expenses** and gave the school $253.00.

a. If books cost $6.00 each, how many books can the school buy with his donation?

b. Will there be any money left over?

Counting Cakes

Ada is making cupcakes for a bake sale. Her recipe makes 25 cupcakes in a batch.

Solve It!

a. If Ada wants to sell 150 cupcakes, how many batches will she need to make?

b. Ada wants to sell the cupcakes in trays that hold 4 cupcakes each. How many trays of cupcakes will she be able to sell? Will she have any cupcakes left over?

c. If Ada sells each tray of cakes for $2.00, how much money will she make?

Use these steps to help you solve the problems.

Step 1: Work out how many batches of cupcakes Ada will need to make 150 cupcakes.

Step 2: Work out how many trays of 4 cupcakes Ada will be able to sell.

Step 3: Find out if there are any cupcakes left over. Write the answer with the remainder as a fraction.

Step 4: Work out how much money Ada will make if she sells all her trays of cupcakes.

Glossary

amounts—quantities

baker—a person whose job is baking bread

bakery—a store where bread is baked and sold

division—a mathematical operation where a number is grouped into equal parts

equation—a mathematical statement to show that two amounts are equal

expenses—costs

fraction—part of a group, number, or whole set

ingredients—the foods needed to make a recipe

multiplication—a mathematical operation where a number is added to itself many times

recipe—instructions for cooking something

Index

baker, 5

bakery, 5, 7, 9

batch, 7, 8, 13, 18, 22–23, 28–29

bread, 5, 6

dozen, 7, 18, 20

ingredients, 9, 10, 12, 14, 16–17, 18, 25

library, 4, 26, 27

money, 4, 17, 25, 27

muffins, 6–8, 9–11, 12, 13, 15, 19–23, 24–27

oven, 7, 11, 18, 22

recipe, 7, 8, 9, 12, 13

savings, 16, 25, 26

school, 4, 24, 26, 27

tins, 8, 11, 20, 21, 22

Let's Explore Math

Page 5:
a. $9.00 ÷ $2.00 = 4 loaves of bread with $1.00 left over
b. $12.00 ÷ $2.00 = 6 loaves of bread
c. $19.00 ÷ $2.00 = 9 loaves of bread with $1.00 left over

Page 7:
a. 12 batches × 12 muffins = 144 muffins

Page 11:
a. $(3 \times 5) + 3$
e. $(10 \times 2) + 1$

Page 15:

a.

$$
\begin{array}{r}
3\,R\,1 \\
3\overline{)\,10} \\
-9 \\
\hline
1 \\
1\tfrac{1}{3}
\end{array}
$$

b.

$$
\begin{array}{r}
2\,R\,2 \\
5\overline{)\,12} \\
-10 \\
\hline
2 \\
2\tfrac{2}{5}
\end{array}
$$

Page 19:
Answers will vary but could include: $4 \times 6 = 24$; $24 ÷ 4 = 6$; $6 \times 8 = 48$; $48 ÷ 8 = 6$

Page 23:
c. $(2 \times 48) + 48$

Page 25:
a. 144 muffins × $3.00 = $432.00
b. 144 muffins × $2.50 = $360.00

Page 27:
a. $253.00 ÷ $6.00 per book = 42 books
b. Yes, there is $1.00 left over.

Problem-Solving Activity

Step 1: 150 cupcakes ÷ 25 cupcakes per batch = 6 batches

Step 2: 150 cupcakes ÷ 4 cupcakes per tray = 37 trays and 2 remainder cupcakes

Step 3:

$$
\begin{array}{r}
37\,R\,②\\
4\overline{)\,150} \quad \frac{2}{4}\\
-148\\
\hline
2\\
= 37\tfrac{2}{4}
\end{array}
$$

Step 4: $2.00 × 37 = $74.00